The
ULTIMATE
INSULT

The ULTIMATE INSULT

COMPILED BY MARIA LEACH

MICHAEL O'MARA BOOKS LIMITED

This paperback edition published in 2002 by
Michael O'Mara Books Limited
9 Lion Yard
Tremadoc Road
London SW4 7NQ

First published in hardback in 1996 by
Michael O'Mara Books Limited

The publisher identifies Maria Leach as the author of this
work.

ISBN 1-85479-288-1

Designed and typeset by K DESIGN, Winscombe, Somerset

Printed and bound by Cox & Wyman, Reading

CONTENTS

There's something Vichy about the French.
Ivor Novello

Boy meets girl, so what.
Bertolt Brecht

Religion is the venereal disease of mankind.
Henri de Montherlant

If capitalism depended on the intellectual
quality of the Conservative party, it would
end about lunchtime tomorrow.
Tony Benn

I think we may class the lawyer in the
natural history of monsters.
John Keats

Music is essentially useless, as life is.
George Santayana

She ran the gamut of emotions from A to B.
Dorothy Parker on Katharine Hepburn

Television: the bland leading the bland.
Anon

All writers are vain, selfish and lazy, and at the very bottom their motives are a mystery.

George Orwell

I thought men like that shot themselves.

King George V

Golf is a good walk spoiled.
Mark Twain

A vacuum with nipples.
Otto Preminger on Marilyn Monroe

She was the personification of a knitting pattern.
Isabella Forbes

NATIONS

I love New York City. I've got a gun.

Charles Barkley

⚜

This is the most exciting place in the world to live. There are so many ways to die here.

Denis Leary on New York City

⚜

Poland is now a totally independent nation, and it has managed to greatly improve its lifestyle thanks to the introduction of modern Western conveniences such as food.

Dave Barry

⚜

The difference between Los Angeles and yogurt is that yogurt has real culture.

Tom Taussik

⚜

I look upon Switzerland as an inferior sort of Scotland.

Sydney Smith

❧❦❧

Life is too short to learn German.

Richard Porson

❧❦❧

Few things can be less tempting or dangerous than a Greek woman of the age of thirty.

John Carne

❧❦❧

What they are they were; and what they were they are – an indolent, careless and mimetic people, but without a spark of Turkish fire, without a touch of Grecian taste. With neither personal restlessness nor pride of origin – with neither large aspirations nor practical dexterity of hand.

W. Hepworth Dixon on British Cyprus, 1887

❧❦❧

Poor Mexico, so far from God and so near to the United States!

Porfirio Diaz

✧◈✧

Realizing that they will never be a world power, the Cypriots have decided to be a world nuisance.

George Mikes

✧◈✧

The trouble with Ireland is that it's a country full of genius, but with absolutely no talent.

Hugh Leonard

❧❦❧

The Irish are a fair people – they never speak well of one another.

Samuel Johnson

❧❦❧

The Koreans have been called 'The Irish of the East', but this is an insult to the Irish.

James Kirkup, Streets of Asia

❧❦❧

German is the most extravagantly ugly language –
it sounds like someone using a sick bag on a 747.

Willy Rushton

❧❧❧

The Serbian countrymen came over as a gang of
brutal yokels with a cultural life only marginally
richer than that of Neanderthal.man.

John Naughton, Observer

❧❧❧

The food in Yugoslavia is fine if you like pork
tartare.

Ed Begley, Jr

❧❧❧

It is absurd to say that there are neither ruins nor
curiosities in America, when they have their
mothers and their manners.

Oscar Wilde

❧❧❧

Of course, America had often been discovered before Columbus, but it had always been hushed up.

Oscar Wilde

The English think soap is civilization.

Heinrich von Treitschke

❦

Britain is the only country in the world where being 'too clever by half' is an insult.

A. A. Gill, Tatler

❦

Italy, at least, has two things to balance its miserable poverty and mismanagement: a lively intellectual movement and a good climate. Ireland is Italy without these two.

James Joyce

❦

Ireland has the honour of being the only country which never persecuted the Jews – because she never let them in.

James Joyce

❦

German is a language which was developed solely to afford the speaker the opportunity to spit at strangers under the guise of polite conversation.

National Lampoon

One thing I will say for the Germans, they are always perfectly willing to give somebody else's land to somebody else.

Will Rogers

I find it hard to say, because when I was there it seemed to be shut.

Clement Freud's impressions on New Zealand

The French are sawed-off sissies who eat snails and slugs and cheese that smells like people's feet. Utter cowards who force their own children to drink wine, they gibber like baboons even when you try to speak to them in their own wimpy language.

P. J. O'Rourke

The ignorance of French society gives one a rough sense of the infinite.

Joseph E. Renan

ಞ಄಄ಞ

They are a short, blue-vested people who carry their own onions when cycling abroad, and have a yard which is 3.37 inches longer than other people's.

Alan Coren on the French

ಞ಄಄ಞ

The English have an extraordinary ability for flying into a great calm.

Alexander Woollcott

ಞ಄಄ಞ

France is a dog-hole.

William Shakespeare, All's Well That Ends Well

ಞ಄಄ಞ

Nobody can simply bring together a country that has 365 kinds of cheeses.

Charles de Gaulle on France

England is a nation of shopkeepers.

Napoleon Bonaparte

Frenchmen resemble apes, who, climbing up a tree from branch to branch, never cease going till they come to the highest branch, and there show their bare behinds.

Michel Eyquem de Montaigne

There are few virtues which the Poles do not possess and there are few errors they have ever avoided.

Winston Churchill

I showed my appreciation of my native land in the usual Irish way by getting out of it as soon as I possibly could.

George Bernard Shaw

America is a large, friendly dog in a very small room. Every time it wags its tail it knocks over a chair.

Arnold Toynbee

Canada is a country so square that even the female impersonators are women.

Richard Brenner

∞

Americans are broad-minded people. They'll accept the fact that a person can be an alcoholic, a dope fiend and a wife beater, and even a newspaperman, but if a man doesn't drive there's something wrong with him.

Art Buchwald

∞

It was wonderful to find America, but it would have been more wonderful to miss it.

Mark Twain

∞

India is an abstraction . . . India is no more a political personality than Europe. India is a geographical term. It is no more a united nation than the Equator.

Winston Churchill

∞

I don't greatly admire Japanese women; they have no figures to speak of, and look as if a bee had stung them in the eye.

Crosbie Garstin, The Dragon and the Lotus

❧❧❧

America is a mistake, a giant mistake!

Sigmund Freud

❧❧❧

America is the only nation in history which miraculously has gone from barbarism to degeneration without the usual interval of civilization.

Georges Clemenceau

❧❧❧

In any world menu, Canada must be considered the vichyssoise of nations. It's cold, half-French, and difficult to stir.

Stuart Keate

❧❧❧

There's something Vichy about the French.

Ivor Novello

France, though armed to the teeth, is pacifist to the core.

Winston Churchill

In America, only the successful writer is important, in France all writers are important, in England no writer is important, and in Australia you have to explain what a writer is.

Geoffrey Cottrell

California is a mess. Closet neuroticism is all very well; elevated to an art form it's rather tiresome.

Michael Watkins

In America sex is an obsession, in other parts of the world it is a fact.

Marlene Dietrich

17

The Americans don't really understand what's going on in Bosnia. To them it's the unspellables killing the unpronouncables.

P. J. O'Rourke, The Sun

⏤⏤❧❦☙⏤⏤

There's no underestimating the intelligence of the American public.

H. L. Mencken

⏤⏤❧❦☙⏤⏤

No one can be as calculatedly rude as the British, which amazes Americans, who do not understand studied insult and can only offer abuse as a substitute.

Paul Gallico

⏤⏤❧❦☙⏤⏤

There have been many definitions of hell, but for the English the best definition is that it is the place where the Germans are the police, the Swedish are the comedians, the Italians are the defence force, Frenchmen dig the roads, the Belgians are the pop singers, the Spanish run the railways, the Turks cook the food, the Irish are the waiters, the Greeks run the Government, and the common language is Dutch.

David Frost and Anthony Jay

❧⊙❧

The English think incompetence is the same thing as sincerity.

Quentin Crisp

❧⊙❧

Germany, the diseased world's bathhouse.

Mark Twain

❧⊙❧

They aren't much good at fighting wars any more. Despite their reputation for fashion, their women have spindly legs. Their music is sappy. But they do know how to whip up a plate of grub.

Mike Royko on the French

⮜◈⮞

I mean, who would want to live in a place where the only cultural advantage is that you can turn right on a red light?

Woody Allen on London

⮜◈⮞

Switzerland is a curst, selfish, swinish country of brutes, placed in the most romantic region of the world.

Lord Byron

⮜◈⮞

The English never smash in a face. They merely refrain from asking it to dinner.

Margaret Halsey

⮜◈⮞

The English instinctively admire any man who has no talent and is modest about it.

James Agate

❧❧❧

England has forty-two religions and only two sauces.

Voltaire

❧❧❧

There's nothing wrong with Southern California that a rise in the ocean level wouldn't cure.

Ross MacDonald

❧❧❧

In California everyone goes to a therapist, is a therapist, or is a therapist going to a therapist.

Truman Capote

❧❧❧

It is a scientific fact that if you stay in California you lose one point off your IQ every year.

Truman Capote

∽◦∞◦∾

If you stay in Beverly Hills too long you become a Mercedes.

Robert Redford

∽◦∞◦∾

RELATIONSHIPS

I like men to behave like men – strong and childish.

Françoise Sagan

❧

A man is like a phonograph with half a dozen records. You soon get tired of them all; and yet you have to sit at the table whilst he reels them off to every new visitor.

George Bernard Shaw

❧

My husband's mind is like a Welsh railway – one track and dirty.

Anon

❧

A man in love is incomplete until he has married. Then he's finished.

Zsa Zsa Gabor

❧

Women are like elephants to me – I like to look at 'em, but I wouldn't want to own one.

W. C. Fields

A woman occasionally is quite a serviceable substitute for masturbation. It takes an abundance of imagination, to be sure.

Karl Kraus

There are two tragedies in life. One is to lose your heart's desire. The other is to gain it.

George Bernard Shaw

Women don't smoke after sex because one drag a night is enough.

Anon

Woman would be more charming if one could fall into her arms without falling into her hands.

Ambrose Bierce

⟋⟍⟋⟍⟋

The fastest way to a man's heart is through his chest.

Roseanne Barr

⟋⟍⟋⟍⟋

Women should be obscene and not heard.

Groucho Marx

What's the definition of a tragedy?
Marrying a man for love and then discovering that
he has no money.

Anon

There's nothing so similar to one poodle dog as
another poodle dog, and that goes for women too.

Pablo Picasso

Sex with a man is all right, but it's not as good as
the real thing.

Anon

I hate women because they always know where things are.

James Thurber

❧❧❧

Whatever women do they must do twice as well as men to be thought half as good. Luckily this is not difficult.

Charlotte Whitton

❧❧❧

Men fantasize about being in bed with two women. Women fantasize about it too because at least they'll have someone to talk to when he falls asleep.

Anon

❧❧❧

Men are creatures with two legs and eight hands.

Jayne Mansfield

❧❧❧

My wife and I tried two or three times in the last forty years to have breakfast together, but it was so disagreeable we had to stop.

Winston Churchill

⤳⦿⦿⦿⤶

The prostitute is the only honest woman left in America.

Ti-Grace Atkinson

⤳⦿⦿⦿⤶

Never feel remorse for what you have thought about your wife. She has thought much worse things about you.

Jean Rostand

❦

She got her good looks from her father. He's a plastic surgeon.

Groucho Marx

❦

Most women are not so young as they are painted.

Max Beerbohm

❦

Sex: the thing that takes up the least amount of time and causes the most amount of trouble.

John Barrymore

❦

Free verse is like free love; it's a contradiction in terms.

G. K. Chesterton

Husbands never become good; they merely become proficient.

H. L. Mencken

The majority of husbands remind me of an orang-utan trying to play the violin.

Honoré de Balzac

All this fuss about sleeping together. For physical pleasure I'd sooner go to my dentist any day.

Evelyn Waugh

A husband is what's left of the lover once the nerve has been extracted.

Helen Rowland

A woman will flirt with anybody in the world as long as other people are looking on.

Oscar Wilde

Boy meets girl, so what?

Bertolt Brecht

His mother should have thrown him away and kept the stork.

Mae West

The husband who wants a happy marriage should learn to keep his mouth shut and his cheque book open.

Groucho Marx

◆◆◆

Certain women should be struck regularly like gongs.

Noël Coward, Private Lives

◆◆◆

Winston, if I were married to you, I'd put poison in your coffee.
Nancy Astor

Nancy, if you were my wife, I'd drink it.
Winston Churchill

I married beneath me, all women do.

Nancy Astor

୰ଊଈ

Marriage is a great institution, but I'm not ready
for an institution.

Mae West

୰ଊଈ

Women have a wonderful sense of right and wrong,
but little sense of right and left.

Don Herold

୰ଊଈ

The trouble with Ian is that he gets off with
women because he can't get on with them.

Rosamond Lehmann on Ian Fleming

୰ଊଈ

The more I see of men, the more I like dogs.

Germaine de Staël

୰ଊଈ

35

A woman will always sacrifice herself if you give her the opportunity. It's her favourite form of self-indulgence.

W. Somerset Maugham

∾⊙∾

The surest way to be alone is to get married.

Gloria Steinem

∾⊙∾

Bigamy is having one husband too many. Monogamy is the same.

Anon (quoted in Fear of Flying, *Erica Jong)*

∾⊙∾

Give a man a free hand and he'll run it all over you.

Mae West

∾⊙∾

Take a close-up of a woman past sixty. You might as well use a picture of a relief map of Ireland!

Nancy Astor (attrib.)

❧❧❧

Nature intended women to be our slaves . . . they are our property; we are not theirs. They belong to us, just as a tree that bears fruit belongs to a gardener. What a mad idea to demand equality for women! Women are nothing but machines for producing children.

Napoleon Bonaparte

❧❧❧

On one issue, at least, men and women agree: they both distrust women.

H. L. Mencken

❧❧❧

Women have many faults, men have only two: everything they say, and everything they do.

Anon

❧❧❧

The charms of a passing woman are usually in direct relation to the speed of her passing.

Marcel Proust

❦

When a woman inclines to learning there is usually something wrong with her sexual apparatus.

Friedrich W. Nietzsche

❦

Girls bored me – they still do. I love Mickey Mouse more than any woman I've ever known.

Walt Disney

❦

Women give us solace, but if it were not for women we should never need solace.

Don Herold

❦

Never trust a man who combs his hair straight from his left armpit.

Alice Roosevelt Longworth

ᨏᨏᨏ

We stay together, but we distrust one another. Ah, yes . . . but isn't that a definition of marriage?

Malcom Bradbury, The History Man

ᨏᨏᨏ

Sex is the biggest nothing of all time.

Andy Warhol

ᨏᨏᨏ

It takes your enemy and your friend, working together, to hurt you: the one to slander you, and the other to bring the news to you.

Mark Twain

ᨏᨏᨏ

The only really happy folk are married women and single men.

H. L. Mencken

❧❧❧

Love is the delightful interval between meeting a beautiful girl and discovering that she looks like a haddock.

John Barrymore

❧❧❧

Love . . . the delusion that one woman differs from another.

H. L. Mencken

❧❧❧

Bride, *n*. A woman with a fine prospect of happiness behind her.

Ambrose Bierce

❧❧❧

Chastity: the most unnatural of the sexual perversions.

Aldous Huxley

A woman drove me to drink, and I never even had the courtesy to thank her.

W. C. Fields

Every time a friend succeeds, I die a little.

Gore Vidal

May God defend me from my friends; I can defend myself from my enemies.

Albert Camus

❧

The one thing your friends will never forgive you is your happiness.

Albert Camus

❧

It is well, when judging a friend, to remember that he is judging you with the same godlike and superior impartiality.

Arnold Bennett

❧

The reason that lovers never weary of each other is because they are always talking about themselves.

François de la Rochefoucauld

❧

Marriage is like paying an endless visit in your worst clothes.

J. B. Priestley

❧❧❧

The dread of loneliness is greater than the fear of bondage, so we get married.

Cyril Connolly

❧❧❧

A friendship recognized by the police.

Robert Louis Stevenson on marriage

❧❧❧

Don't knock masturbation – it's sex with someone I love.

Woody Allen

❧❧❧

Love: a burnt match skating in a urinal.

Hart Crane

❧❧❧

I can understand companionship. I can understand bought sex in the afternoon. I cannot understand the love affair.

Gore Vidal

❦

Since the law prohibits the keeping of wild animals and I get no enjoyment from pets, I prefer to remain unmarried.

Karl Kraus

❦

The pleasure is momentary, the position ridiculous, and the expense damnable.

Lord Chesterfield on sex

❦

A woman without a man is like a fish without a bicycle.

Gloria Steinem

❦

The allurement that women hold out to men is precisely the allurement that Cape Hatteras holds out to sailors: they are enormously dangerous and hence enormously fascinating.

H. L. Mencken

Never try to impress a woman, because if you do she'll expect you to keep up to the standard for the rest of your life.

W. C. Fields

The music at a wedding procession always reminds me of the music of soldiers going into battle.

Heinrich Heine

The comfortable estate of widowhood is the only hope that keeps up a wife's spirits.

John Gay

Love is two minutes fifty-two seconds of squishing noises. It shows your mind isn't clicking right.

Johnny Rotten

⊷⊶

Love, in present day society, is just the exchange of two momentary desires and the contact of two skins.

Nicolas-Sebastien Chamfort

⊷⊶

Love as a relation between men and women was ruined by the desire to make sure of the legitimacy of children.

Bertrand Russell

⊷⊶

A promiscuous person is someone who is getting more sex than you are.

Victor Lownes

⊷⊶

Romance should never begin with sentiment. It should begin with science and end with a settlement.

Oscar Wilde

⊷⊶

First love is a kind of vaccination which saves a man from catching the complaint a second time.

Honoré de Balzac

⊷⊶

People who are not in love fail to understand how an intelligent man can suffer because of a very ordinary woman. This is like being surprised that anyone should be stricken with cholera because of a creature so insignificant as the common bacillus.

Marcel Proust

⊷⊶

Nothing to me is more distasteful than that entire complacency and satisfaction which beam in the countenance of a newly-married couple.

Charles Lamb

⊷⊶

In the forties, to get a girl you had to be a GI or a jock. In the fifties, to get a girl you had to be Jewish. In the sixties, to get a girl you had to be black. In the seventies, to get a girl you've got to be a girl.

Mort Sahl

RELIGION

All religions are founded on the fear of the many
and the cleverness of the few.

Henri Beyle Stendhal

Many people think they have religion when they
are troubled with dyspepsia.

Robert G. Ingersoll, Liberty of Man, Woman and Child

Religion is the venereal disease of mankind.

Henri de Montherlant

There is only one race greater than the Jews – and
that is the Derby.

Victor Sassoon

My dear child, you must believe in God inspite of
what the clergy tell you.

Benjamin Jowett

Puritanism – the haunting fear that someone, somewhere, may be happy.

H. L. Mencken

⌘

Religion is the fashionable substitute for belief.

Oscar Wilde

⌘

[God] invented the giraffe, the elephant and the cat. He has no real style. He just goes on trying other things.

Pablo Picasso

⌘

Forgive, O Lord, my little jokes on Thee
And I'll forgive Thy great big one on me.

Robert Frost

⌘

Religion is a monumental chapter in the history of human egotism.

William James

❧⊱❧

An honest God is the noblest work of man.

Robert G. Ingersoll, The Gods

❧⊱❧

The cosmos is a gigantic flywheel, making 10,000 revolutions a minute. Man is a sick fly taking a dizzy ride on it. Religion is the theory that the wheel was designed and set spinning to give him the ride.

H. L. Mencken

❧⊱❧

Operationally, God is beginning to resemble not a ruler but the last fading smile of a Cheshire cat.

Julian Huxley, Religion without Revelation

❧⊱❧

The impotence of God is infinite.

Anatole France

⌒⌒⌒

Heaven, as conventionally conceived, is a place so inane, so dull, so useless, so miserable, that nobody has ever ventured to describe a whole day in heaven, though plenty of people have described a day at the seaside.

George Bernard Shaw

⌒⌒⌒

In heaven all the interesting people are missing.

Friedrich W. Nietzsche

⌒⌒⌒

When I think of the number of disagreeable people that I know who have gone to a better world, I am sure hell won't be so bad at all.

Mark Twain

⌒⌒⌒

Man is a dog's ideal of what God should be.

Holbrook Jackson

❧❧❧

Perhaps the most revolting character that the
United States ever produced was the Christian
businessman.

H. L. Mencken

The Bible tells us to love our neighbours, and also to love our enemies; probably because they are generally the same people.

G. K. Chesterton

The inspiration of the Bible depends on the ignorance of the gentleman who reads it.

Robert G. Ingersoll

The trouble with born-again Christians is that they are an even bigger pain the second time around.

Herb Caen

We must respect the other fellow's religion, but only in the sense and to the extent that we respect his theory that his wife is beautiful and his children smart.

H. L. Mencken

You never see animals going through the absurd and often horrible fooleries of magic and religion. Only man behaves with such gratuitous folly. It is the price he has to pay for being intelligent but not, as yet, quite intelligent enough.

Aldous Huxley

A Sunday school is a prison in which children do penance for the evil conscience of their parents.

H. L. Mencken

❧❧❧

The believer is happy; the doubter is wise.

Hungarian proverb

❧❧❧

Archbishop: a Christian ecclesiastic of a rank superior to that attained by Christ.

H. L. Mencken

❧❧❧

Scriptures, *n*. The sacred books of our holy religion, as distinguished from the false and profane writings on which all other faiths are based.

Ambrose Bierce

❧❧❧

The Holy Roman Empire was neither holy, nor Roman, nor an Empire.

Voltaire

❧❧❧

People may say what they like about the decay of
Christianity; the religious system that produced
green Chartreuse can never really die.

Saki

✦

Organized Christianity has probably done more to
retard the ideals that were its founder's than any
other agency in the world.

Richard Le Gallienne

✦

Self-denial is the shiny sore on the leprous body of
Christianity.

Oscar Wilde

✦

Truth, in matters of religion, is simply the opinion
that has survived.

Oscar Wilde

✦

Going to church doesn't make you a Christian any more than going to the garage makes you a car.

Laurence J. Peter

◦◦◦◦

People in general are equally horrified at hearing the Christian religion doubted, and at seeing it practised.

Samuel Butler

◦◦◦◦

Confession is good for the soul only in the sense that a tweed coat is good for dandruff – it is a palliative rather than a remedy.

Peter de Vries

◦◦◦◦

A casual stroll through the lunatic asylums shows that faith does not prove anything.

Friedrich W. Nietsche

◦◦◦◦

Beware of the man whose God is in the skies.

George Bernard Shaw

The Christian ideal has not been tried and found wanting; it has been found difficult and left untried.

G. K. Chesterton

He's a born-again Christian. The trouble is, he suffered brain damage during rebirth.

Anon

I cannot believe in a God who wants to be praised all the time.

Friedrich W. Nietzsche

God seems to have left the receiver off the hook and time is running out.

Arthur Koestler

I admire the serene assurance of those who have religious faith. It is wonderful to observe the calm confidence of a Christian with four aces.

Mark Twain

❧❧❧

God, that dumping ground of our dreams.

Jean Rostand

❧❧❧

If you talk to God, you are praying; if God talks to you, you have schizophrenia.

Thomas Szasz

❧❧❧

I do not believe in God. I believe in cashmere.

Fran Lebowitz

❧❧❧

The Christian religion not only was at first attended with miracles, but even at this day cannot be believed by any reasonable person without one.

David Hume

❧❧❧

Christ: an anarchist who succeeded. That's all.

Friedrich W. Nietzsche

Which is it: is man one of God's blunders, or is God one of man's blunders?

Friedrich W. Nietzsche

God is the celebrity-author of the world's bestseller. We have made God into the biggest celebrity of all, to contain our own emptiness.

Daniel Boorstin

The chief contribution of Protestantism to human thought is its massive proof that God is a bore.

H. L. Mencken

෴

There is only one honest impulse at the bottom of Puritanism, and that is the impulse to punish the man with a superior capacity for happiness.

H. L. Mencken

෴

The last Christian died on the cross.

Friedrich W. Nietzsche

෴

If God created us in his own image, we have more than reciprocated.

Voltaire

෴

Faith may be defined briefly as an illogical belief in the occurrence of the improbable.

H. L. Mencken

෴

POLITICS

There are two things I don't like about you, Mr Churchill – your politics and your moustache.

My dear madam, pray do not disturb yourself. You are not likely to come in contact with either.

Winston Churchill responding to an insult

❧

If capitalism depended on the intellectual quality of the Conservative party, it would end about lunchtime tomorrow.

Tony Benn

❧

The mistake a lot of politicians make is forgetting they've been appointed, and thinking they've been anointed.

Mrs Claude Pepper

❧

The only thing he ever took up at university was space.

Anon on Denis Healey

❧

Politics is the art of looking for trouble, finding it everywhere, diagnosing it wrongly, and applying unsuitable remedies.

Ernest Benn

We know that he has, more than any other man, the gift of compressing the largest amount of words into the smallest amount of thought.

Winston Churchill on Ramsay Macdonald

༄ঞ্চ৩৩

Winston had devoted the best years of his life to preparing his impromptu speeches.

F. E. Smith on Winston Churchill

༄ঞ্চ৩৩

He is a man suffering from petrified adolescence.

Aneurin Bevan on Winston Churchill

༄ঞ্চ৩৩

Dear Randolph, utterly unspoiled by failure.

Noël Coward on Randolph Churchill

༄ঞ্চ৩৩

A triumph of modern science to find the only part of Randolph that was not malignant and remove it.

Evelyn Waugh on Randolph Churchill

༄ঞ্চ৩৩

The Right Honourable gentleman's smile is like the fittings on a coffin.

Benjamin Disraeli on Sir Robert Peel

❧❧❧

A politician is a person with whose politics you don't agree; if you agree with him he is a statesman.

David Lloyd George

❧❧❧

He has not a single redeeming defect.

Benjamin Disraeli on William Gladstone

❧❧❧

Posterity will do justice to that unprincipled maniac ... with his extraordinary mixture of envy, vindictiveness, hypocrisy and superstition; and with his one commanding characteristic – whether Prime Minister or Leader of the Opposition, whether preaching, praying, speechifying or scribbling – never a gentleman.

Benjamin Disraeli on William Gladstone

❧❧❧

If you weren't such a great man you'd be a terrible bore.

Mrs William Gladstone to her husband

⤞⟨◉⟩⤝

He'll double-cross that bridge when he comes to it.

Oscar Levant on a politician

⤞⟨◉⟩⤝

My deepest feeling about politicians is that they are dangerous lunatics to be avoided when possible and carefully humoured; people, above all, to whom one must never tell the truth.

W. H. Auden

⤞⟨◉⟩⤝

A Conservative is a Liberal who has been mugged.

Anon

⤞⟨◉⟩⤝

Conservatives are not necessarily stupid, but most stupid people are Conservatives.

John Stuart Mill

⤞⟨◉⟩⤝

71

A Conservative is a man who is too cowardly to fight and too fat to run.

Albert Hubbard

∿⸙∾

John Major, Norman Lamont: I wouldn't spit in their mouths if their teeth were on fire.

Rodney Bickerstaffe, UNISON

∿⸙∾

That poisonous lady with the poisonous tongue.

John Junor, Mail on Sunday, *on Edwina Currie*

∿⸙∾

She is the Castro of the Western world – an embarrassment to her friends – all she lacks is a beard.

Denis Healey on Margaret Thatcher

∿⸙∾

He delivers all his statements as though auditioning for the speaking clock.

Stephen Glover, Evening Standard, *on John Major*

∿⸙∾

The Monarch of Muddle Through.

Simon Jenkins, The Times, *on John Major*

❧❧❧

John Major is to leadership what Cyril Smith is to hang-gliding.

John Prescott

❧❧❧

Major is what he is: a man from nowhere, going nowhere, heading for well-merited obscurity as fast as his mediocre talents can carry him.

Paul Johnson, Spectator

❧❧❧

A semi-house-trained polecat.

Michael Foot on Norman Tebbit

❦❧❦❧

Attila the Hen.

Clement Freud on Margaret Thatcher

❦❧❦❧

The Prime Minister tells us that she has given the French president a piece of her mind – not a gift I would receive with alacrity.

Denis Healey on Margaret Thatcher

❦

She's a handbag economist who believes that you pay as you go.

New Yorker *on Margaret Thatcher*

❦

He looked like a tall, blond marionette on a jerky string.

Paul Callan, Daily Express, *on Michael Heseltine*

❦

His delivery at the dispatch-box has all the bite of a rubber duck.

Marcia Falkender on John Moore

❦

Lady Fork-Bender.

Private Eye *on Marcia Falkender*

❦

Politics is the diversion of trivial men who, when
they succeed at it, become important in the eyes of
more trivial men.

George Jean Nathan

All politics are based on the indifference of the majority.

James Reston

⤛⤜⤛⤜

The only thing I really mind about going to prison is the thought of Lord Longford visiting me.

Richard Ingrams

⤛⤜⤛⤜

It is a pity, as my husband says, that more politicians are not bastards by birth instead of vocation.

Katherine Whitehorn

⤛⤜⤛⤜

Don't you ever talk like that to me again. I'll have your head off your shoulders, and the skin off your back.

Michael Foot to Roy Hattersley

⤛⤜⤛⤜

You couldn't knock the skin off a rice pudding.

Roy Hattersley to Michael Foot

⤛⤜⤛⤜

A good politician is quite as unthinkable as an honest burglar.

H. L. Mencken

Not even her best friends would describe her as a glamour puss, whose face would be likely to turn on many voters. Except perhaps those who are members of the British Horse Society.

John Junor, Mail on Sunday, *on Margaret Beckett*

Far better to keep your mouth shut and let everyone think you're stupid than to open it and leave no doubt.

Norman Tebbit on Dennis Skinner

⤞◈⤝

The Bertie Wooster of Marxism.

Anon on Tony Benn

⤞◈⤝

A prissy, pompous little bantam-cock of a man.

John Junor, Mail on Sunday, *on John Smith*

⤞◈⤝

He has the consistency of the chameleon and the wisdom of the weathercock.

Michael Howard on Neil Kinnock

⤞◈⤝

That great bloated unsmiling accuser.

Philip Larkin on Roy Hattersley

⤞◈⤝

79

The dismal-voiced, dough-faced and discredited twister.

Andrew Marr, Independent, *on Harold Wilson*

✤

Every government carries a health warning.

Anon

✤

I saw David Owen on television the other week. He was heckling a small number of bystanders in Torquay. And then I realized they weren't bystanders – they were his own party.

Kenneth Baker on David Owen

✤

They are not so much a party, more like a disease.

David Owen on Liberal Democrats

✤

If God had been a Liberal, there wouldn't have been ten commandments, there would have been ten suggestions.

Malcolm Bradbury and Christopher Bigsby, After Dinner Game

✤

His boyish charm has begun to petrify into an empty adolescent grin. At his press conferences, you expect the first question to be, 'Is there anybody in?'

Keith Waterhouse, Daily Mail, *on Paddy Ashdown*

Being in politics is like being a football coach; you have to be smart enough to understand the game, and dumb enough to think it's important.

Eugene McCarthy

∽◑◐◑◐∾

The enviably attractive nephew who sings an Irish ballad for the company and then winsomely disappears before the table-clearing and dish-washing began.

Lyndon B. Johnson on John F. Kennedy

∽◑◐◑◐∾

Gerry Ford is so dumb that he can't fart and chew gum at the same time.

Lyndon B. Johnson on Gerald Ford

∽◑◐◑◐∾

Don't be so humble. You're not that great.

Golda Meir to Moshe Dayan

∽◑◐◑◐∾

Nixon's motto was: If two wrongs don't make a right, try three.

Norman Cousins on Richard Nixon

❦

Nixon is a no-good lying bastard. He can lie out of both sides of his mouth at the same time, and even if he caught himself telling the truth, he'd lie just to keep his hand in.

Harry S. Truman

❦

When Carter gave a fireside chat, the fire went out.

Anon on Jimmy Carter

❦

He doesn't dye his hair – he's just prematurely orange.

Gerald Ford on Ronald Reagan

❦

A senescent bimbo with a lust for home furnishings.

Barbara Ehrenreich on Nancy Reagan

❦

Bill Clinton is a dope-smoking, draft-dodging liar, whose wife never knows where he is.

Anti-Clinton rally placard

❧

That smiling barracuda.

US National Review *on Hilary Clinton*

❧

The left in Canada is more gauche than sinister.

John Harney

❧

For Socialists, going to bed with the Liberals is like having oral sex with a shark.

Larry Zolf

❧

He skilfully avoided what was wrong without saying what was right and never let his on the one hand know what his on the other hand was doing.

Frank Scott on W. L. Mackenzie King

❧

PROFESSIONS:
LEGAL & GENERAL

Beneath this smooth stone by the bone of his bone
Sleeps Master John Gill;
By lies when alive this attorney did thrive,
And now that he's dead he lies still.

Epitaph for a lawyer, anon

∽⦁⦁⦁∽

If that be law, I'll go home and burn my books.

Lord Mansfield

My Lord, you'd better go home and read them.

Lord Ashburton

∽⦁⦁⦁∽

It has been said that there are seven essential
requisites for going to law: a good cause, a good
lawyer, good evidence, good witnesses, a good
judge, a good jury, and good luck!

Anon

∽⦁⦁⦁∽

For certain people, after fifty, litigation takes the place of sex.

Gore Vidal

∞

To call him grey would be an insult to porridge.

Sir Nicholas Fairbairn on Scottish judge, Lord Hope

∞

She's a good lawyer, but 'finesse' and Marcia Clark should not be used in the same sentence.

Henry Weinstein, Los Angeles Times, *on the Chief Prosecutor in the O. J. Simpson trial*

∞

He has had his fifteen minutes of fame, which is more than he deserves. Let us now put him back in his box.

Lynn Barber, Independent on Sunday, *on Judge James Pickles*

∞

From Lord Hailsham we have heard a virtuoso performance in the art of kicking a fallen friend in the guts. . .. When self-indulgence has reduced a man to the shape of Lord Hailsham, sexual continence involves no more than a sense of the ridiculous.

Anon, commentary on Lord Hailsham's censure of John Profumo

Judges are apt to be naive, simple-minded men.

Oliver Wendell Holmes

Judges, as a class, display, in a matter of arranging alimony, that reckless generosity which is found only in men who are giving away someone else's cash.

P. G. Wodehouse

I have come to regard the law-courts not as a cathedral but rather as a casino.

Richard Ingrams, Guardian

No brilliance is needed in the law. Nothing but common sense and relatively clean fingernails.

John Mortimer, A Voyage Round My Father

꧁꧂

Law is a bottomless pit, it is a cormorant, a harpy that devours everything.

Jonathan Swift

꧁꧂

Lawyer, *n*. One skilled in the circumvention of the law.

Lawsuit, *n*. A machine which you go into as a pig and come out of as a sausage.

Ambrose Bierce

꧁꧂

Lawyers, I suppose were children once.

Charles Lamb.

꧁꧂

91

I do not come to speak ill of any man behind his back, but I believe the gentleman is an attorney.

Samuel Johnson.

<hr>

'There is a rogue at the end of my cane.'

... 'At which end, my lord?'

Judge Jeffreys pointing at a rebel at the Bloody Assizes.

<hr>

Laws are generally found to be nets of such a texture, as the little creep through, the great break through, and the middle-sized are alone entangled in.

William Shenstone

<hr>

A jury consists of twelve persons chosen to decide who has the better lawyer.

Robert Frost

<hr>

You will die either on the gallows, or of the pox.

Lord Sandwich

'. . . that must depend on whether I embrace your
lordship's principles or your mistress.'

Samuel Foot (attrib.)

⌘

As God is my judge – I am innocent.

Convicted criminal

He isn't; I am, and you're not!

Judge Norman Birkett

⌘

The law, in its majestic equality, forbids the rich as
well as the poor to sleep under bridges, to beg in
the streets, and to steal bread.

Anatole France

⌘

It is absolutely the best example to give anyone to get rid of the judiciary. He is rude, offensive and intolerant.

Anon lawyer, Observer *Magazine, on Mr Justice Harman*

❧❧❧

Lawyers and painters can soon turn white to black.

Danish proverb

❧❧❧

A man who is his own lawyer has a fool for a client.

Anon

A man who is his own lawyer has a fool for a client.

❦

I think we may class the lawyer in the natural history of monsters.

John Keats

❦

Doctors are just the same as lawyers; the only difference is that lawyers merely rob you, whereas doctors rob you and kill you, too.

Anton Chekhov

❦

A doctor's reputation is made by the number of eminent men who die under his care.

George Bernard Shaw

❦

The art of medicine consists in amusing the patient while nature cures the disease.

Voltaire

❦

A plastic surgeon is one who has credit card facilities.

Mike Barfield, The Oldie

❦❧

The best doctor is the one you run for and can't find.

Denis Diderot

❦❧

I've decided to skip 'holistic'. I don't know what it means, and I don't want to know. That may seem extreme, but I followed the same strategy toward 'Gestalt' and the 'Twist', and lived to tell the tale.

Calvin Trillin

❦❧

As a rational scientist, Einstein is a fair violinist. Einstein is already dead and buried alongside Andersen, Grimm and the Mad Hatter.

George F. Gilette on Albert Einstein

❦❧

It is easier to square the circle than to get round a mathematician.

Augustus de Morgan, A Budget of Paradoxes

❦❧

The City is like an orgy where no one stops to have a bath.

Charlie Richardson

∽◦∾

He's called a broker because after you deal with him you are.

Anon

∽◦∾

I find it rather easy to portray a businessman. Being bland, rather cruel and incompetent comes naturally to me.

John Cleese, Newsweek

❧❧❧

I don't like to hire consultants. They're like castrated bulls – all they can do is advise.

Victor Kiam, Going for It

❧❧❧

Consultants are people who borrow your watch to tell you the time and then walk off with it.

Robert Townsend

❧❧❧

Actuaries have the reputation of being about as interesting as the footnotes on a pension plan.

George Pitcher

❧❧❧

Auditers are the troops who watch a battle from the safety of a hillside and, when the battle is over, come down to count the dead and bayonet the wounded.

Anon

❧❧❧❧

The Metropolitan Police Force is abbreviated to the MET to give more members a chance of spelling it.

Mike Barfield, The Oldie

❧❧❧❧

Detectives are only policemen with smaller feet.

Whitfield Crook, Stage Fright

❧❧❧❧

Anyone who has been to an English public school and served in the British Army is quite at home in a Third World prison.

Roger Cooper

❧❧❧❧

I am inclined to think that one's education
has been in vain if one fails to learn that most
schoolmasters are idiots.

Hesketh Pearson

∽◦◦◦∾

The schoolteacher is certainly underpaid as a
child-minder, but ludicrously overpaid as an
educator.

John Osborne

∽◦◦◦∾

MUSIC

Music is essentially useless, as life is.

George Santayana

&⟨oΘo⟩∂

Hell is full of musical amateurs. Music is the
brandy of the damned.

George Bernard Shaw

&⟨oΘo⟩∂

I like Wagner's music better than any other music.
It is so loud that one can talk the whole time
without people hearing what one says. That is a
great advantage.

Oscar Wilde

&⟨oΘo⟩∂

I occasionally play works by contemporary
composers and for two reasons. First to discourage
the composer from writing any more, and secondly,
to remind myself how much I appreciate
Beethoven.

Jascha Heifetz

&⟨oΘo⟩∂

Beethoven's imagination in the finale of this quartet suggests a poor swallow flitting incessantly in a hermetically-sealed compartment to the annoyance of our eyes and our ears.

H. Blanchard

❧❀❧

Art is long and life is short: here is evidently the explanation of a Brahms symphony.

Edward Lorne

❧❀❧

Is Wagner a human being at all? Is he not rather a disease?

Friedrich W. Nietzsche

❧❀❧

Wagner writes like an intoxified pig.

George T. Strong

❧❀❧

A composer for one right hand.

Richard Wagner on Frederic Chopin

❧❀❧

Far too noisy, my dear Mozart. Far too many notes.

Archduke Ferdinand

❧❦❧

Wagner's music is better than it sounds.

Mark Twain

❧❦❧

I love Wagner, but the music I prefer is that of a
cat hung up by its tail outside a window and trying
to stick to panes of glass with its claws.

Charles Baudelaire

❧❦❧

Some of his pages resemble a kitchen flypaper
during the rush-hour on a hot August afternoon.

C. W. Orr on Arnold Schoenberg

❧❦❧

Perhaps it was because Nero played the fiddle, they
burned Rome.

Oliver Herford

❧❦❧

A partly formed talent being wholly hyped by partly formed brains.

Christopher Wilson on Vanessa Mae

Wagner has beautiful moments but awful quarter hours.

Gioacchino Antonio Rossini

Strauss may be characterized in four words: little talent, much impudence.

Cesar Cui on Richard Strauss

❧

Why do we have to have all these third-rate foreign conductors around – when we have so many second-rate ones of our own?

Sir Thomas Beecham

❧

Of all noises, I think music is the least disagreeable.

Samuel Johnson

❧

The chief objection to playing wind instruments is that it prolongs the life of the player.

George Bernard Shaw

❧

Opera, *n*. A play representing life in another world whose inhabitants have no speech but song, no motions but gestures, and no postures but attitudes.

Ambrose Bierce

How wonderful opera would be if there were no singers.

Gioacchino Antonio Rossini

When an opera star sings her head off, she usually improves her appearance.

Victor Borge

Opera is a loosely connected series of songs designed to make a full evening's entertainment out of an overture.

Miles Kington

Musical people always want one to be perfectly dumb at the very moment when one is longing to be absolutely deaf.

Oscar Wilde

❧❧❧

The Liberace of the nineties.

John Drummond on Nigel Kennedy

❧❧❧

Liberace is pure art student gone camping.

Peter Freedman, Glad to be Grey

❧❧❧

The man with a voice like a cartoon duck.

Ross Fortune, Time Out, *on Gilbert O'Sullivan*

❧❧❧

Andrew Lloyds-Bank.

Private Eye *on Andrew Lloyd Webber*

❧❧❧

Lloyd Webber's music is everywhere, but so is AIDS.

Malcolm Williamson

❦

He's so worn by experience he's got bags under his head.

Clive James, Observer, *on Charles Aznavour*

❦

He is to piano playing as David Soul is to acting; he makes Jacques Loussier sound like Bach; he reminds us how cheap potent music can be.

Richard Williams on Richard Clayderman

❦

Her work is pretensiously arty, over-involved and over-projected, and made further intolerable by a vital tone best described by the Irish word 'keening'.

John Indcox on Barbra Streisand

❦

I had another dream the other day about music critics. They were small and rodent-like with padlocked ears, as if they had stepped out of a painting by Goya.

Igor Stravinsky

❧❦❧

Brass bands are all very well in their place – outdoors and several miles away.

Sir Thomas Beecham (attrib.)

❧❦❧

Jazz: music invented for the torture of imbeciles.

Henry van Dyke

❧❦❧

Jazz has a bad name because some of it is crap, and it's boring.

Jools Holland, Jazz Express

❧❦❧

Live Jazz – two words which find my hands instinctively shooting up to protect my ears.

Craig Brown, The Sunday Times

∽⟨◈⟩∽

You're a repulsive sweaty-faced lout. Singing love songs. Why, you're past it. Hang your gun up now. And all your dirty jokes leave them to the real comedians. You have a mouth like a duck's ass. You dirty minded oaf. You're a load of rubbish.

Anon letter to George Melly

∽⟨◈⟩∽

Why does Courtney Pine always look like a startled dildo?

Robert Mapplethorpe

❧◈❧

Phonograph, *n*. An irritating toy that restores life to dead noises.

Ambrose Bierce

❧◈❧

Once upon a time, rock music was sung by the young to disgust the old. Now, it seems, it is sung by the old to embarrass the young.

Craig Brown, The Sunday Times

❧◈❧

How could I possibly have a sexual relationship with a fifty-year-old fossil? I have a beautiful boyfriend of twenty-eight . . . why should I swap for a dinosaur?

Carla Bruni on Mick Jagger

❧◈❧

The dullards of rock.

Time Out *on Dire Straits*

❦

Zimmerman? Zimmerframe more like, you useless cactus-faced crock of cack.

Melody Maker *on Bob Dylan*

❦

How is it possible to play the harmonica, professionally, for thirty years and still show no sign of improvement?

David Sinclair, The Times, *on Bob Dylan*

❦

I love his work but I couldn't warm to him even if I was cremated next to him.

Keith Richards on Chuck Berry

❦

He's the Walt Disney of street poets – as useful a social commentator as Donald Duck.

Chris Rea on Bruce Springsteen

❦

He plays four-and-a-half-hour sets. That's torture. Does he hate his audience?

John Lydon on Bruce Springsteen

❧❧❧

That bouffant looks ridiculous; it looks more like a mushroom, for God's sake! But then, this is Gary Glitter, after all, a man unacquainted with taste.

Nick Duerden, Select

❧❧❧

This man forgot how to sound or look natural
thirty years ago.

Dave Jennings, Melody Maker, *on Cliff Richard*

∞◦⊙◦∞

A sort of wiggly-bottomed Mike Baldwin.

Craig Brown, The Sunday Times, *on Rod Stewart*

∞◦⊙◦∞

Rock n' roll is musical baby food: it is the worship
of mediocrity, brought about by a passion for
conformity.

Mitch Miller

∞◦⊙◦∞

Rock is a little boy's playground and little boys
don't talk about anything that women are
interested in or concerned about. Apart from how
big their willies are.

Jo 'Fuzzbox'

∞◦⊙◦∞

The face that launched a thousand whores.

Stud Brothers, Melody Maker, *on Debbie Harry*

❦

He sounds like he's got a brick dangling from his willy, and a food-mixer making purée of his tonsils.

Paul Lester, Melody Maker, *on Jon Bon Jovi*

❦

La Trina Turner – these days she's as tasty and hygienic as a mouthful of Domestos.

Melody Maker *on Tina Turner*

❦

Rhythm and blues is not music, it's a disease.

Mitch Miller

❦

Unspeakable, untalented and vulgar young entertainer.

Bing Crosby on Elvis Presley

❦

This fourth-form philosophizing meander across the fretboards of the consciousness, attempting to be Orwell, ending up being awful.

Melody Maker on Pink Floyd's The Wall

❦

Most posthumous eulogizing of Freddie respectfully touched on what a 'great entertainer' he was. Well, true in part, but then so is Bruce Forsyth.

Dave Morrison, Select, *on Freddie Mercury*

❦

Do we need a two-and-a-half-hour movie about The Doors? I don't think so. I'll sum it up for you. I'M DRUNK – I'M FAMOUS – I'M DRUNK – I'M DEAD. 'Big Fat Dead Guy in a Bathtub', there's your title.

Denis Leary on Jim Morrison, The Doors

❦

Some people exist who like to see their names in print. John Lennon and Yoko Ono are print junkies.

Germaine Greer

❦

No one can compete with McLaren when he is ranting like a highly strung washerwoman about his favourite subject: himself.

James Delingpole, Sunday Telegraph, *on Malcolm McLaren*

🙰🙰🙰

It's kind of like watching a chicken try to fly, you wish it would stop, or turn into a swan, or even just stop trying so hard.

The Stud Brothers, Melody Maker, *on Belinda Carlisle* Leave a Light on

🙰🙰🙰

You only notice a Tracy Chapman record when it ends, like a faint humming in your ear that has suddenly stopped.

Melody Maker

🙰🙰🙰

If music be the food of love, why do the Eurythmics insist on serving up spam and chips all the time?

Pauline, Pluto

🙰🙰🙰

'Old Red Eyes is Back' – more horrid than shit on your pillow.

Melody Maker on *The Beautiful South*

⋘⋙

He sometimes brings out records with the greatest titles in the world, which somewhere along the line he neglects to write songs for.

Elvis Costello on *Morrissey*

⋘⋙

Disco music is a kind of background music that is louder than anything in the foreground.

Miles Kington

⤳◈⤶

That rap stuff is noise pollution.

Kiefer Sutherland

⤳◈⤶

Doesn't Boy George remind you of Su Pollard?

John Lydon

⤳◈⤶

I've seen Bauhaus, so I've seen bad, and I've seen Foreigner, so I've seen worse.

Steve Sutherland, Melody Maker

⤳◈⤶

The boy's got more plastic on him than a Co-op bag.

Melody Maker *on Michael Jackson*

⤳◈⤶

121

Michael Jackson's album was only called 'Bad' because there wasn't enough room on the sleeve for 'Pathetic'.

The Artist Formerly Known as Prince

DRAMATIC ART:
THEATRE & CINEMA

You can take all the sincerity in Hollywood, place it in the navel of a fruit fly and still have room enough for three caraway seeds and a producer's heart.

Fred Allen

❧❧❧

Elizabeth Taylor, sounding something like Minnie Mouse and weighted down to her ankles in comedic intent, keeps crashing against the trees while Richard Burton ... slogs up and down oddly majestic molehills.

Kevin Kelly on the play Private Lives

❧❧❧

Elizabeth Taylor looks like two small boys fighting underneath a thick blanket.

Mr Blackwell, designer

❧❧❧

It only goes to show that when you give the public what it wants, it will turn out.

Attributed to Red Skelton at Louis B. Mayer's funeral

❧❧❧

An associate producer is the only guy in
Hollywood who will associate with a producer.

Fred Allen

❦

If my film makes one more person miserable, I've
done my job.

Woody Allen

❦

Glenda Jackson has a face to launch a thousand dredgers.

Jack de Manio

❧⊷⊷

You always knew where you were with Goldwyn. Nowhere.

F. Scott Fitzgerald on Samuel Goldwyn

❧⊷⊷

In the first of these films, Miss Garland plays herself, which is horrifying; in the second someone else, which is impossible.

John Simon on Judy Garland

❧⊷⊷

A great actress from the waist down.

Dame Margaret Kendal on Sarah Bernhardt

❧⊷⊷

I have more talent in my smallest fart that you have in your entire body.

Walter Matthau to Barbra Streisand

❧⊷⊷

She was good at playing abstract confusion in the same way that a midget is good at being short.

Clive James on Marilyn Monroe

His critiques of films are subtle and can be very amusing, especially of the ones he hasn't seen.

David Hockney on Billy Wilder

Paradise with a lobotomy.

Anon on Hollywood

Hollywood is where the stars twinkle,
then wrinkle.

Victor Mature

Hollywood is a great place to live if you happen to be an orange.

Fred Allen

The only 'ism' Hollywood believes in is plagiarism.

Dorothy Parker

⤜⧜⧝⤛

Alan Ladd had only two expressions: hat on and hat off.

Anon

⤜⧜⧝⤛

A non-descript, adenoidal, weasel-eyed, narrow-chested, stoop-shouldered, repulsive creature with all the outward appearance of a cretin.

Burton Rascoe on William Bonney (a.k.a. Billy the Kid)

⤜⧜⧝⤛

. . . the only person who ever left the Iron Curtain wearing it.

Oscar Levant on Zsa Zsa Gabor

⤜⧜⧝⤛

She ran the gamut of emotions from A to B.

Dorothy Parker on Katharine Hepburn

⤜⧜⧝⤛

Shelley Duval is the worst and homeliest thing to hit the movies since Liza Minnelli.

John Simon

~~~

I suppose he looks all right, if your tastes happen to run to septuagenarians with blow waves and funny stretch marks around the ears.

Lynn Barber on Kirk Douglas

~~~

Chevvy Chase couldn't ad-lib a fart after a baked-bean dinner.

Johnny Carson

~~~

Miss Streisand looks like a cross between an aardvark and an albino rat surmounted by a platinum-coated horse bun.

John Simon on Barbra Streisand

~~~

He looked like a half-melted rubber bulldog.

John Simon on Walter Matthau

Let's face it, Elizabeth Taylor's last marriage was all about selling perfume because it's hard to sell perfume when you're a fat old spinster.

Johnny Rotten

Towards the end of her life she looked like a
hungry insect magnified a million times –
a praying mantis that had forgotten how to pray.

Quentin Crisp on Joan Crawford

The great thing about Errol was that you knew
precisely where you were with him – because he
always let you down.

David Niven on Errol Flynn.

Poor little man. They made him out of lemon
Jell-O and there he is.

Adela Rogers Saint-John on Robert Redford

They should give Haber open-heart surgery – and go in through the feet.

Julie Andrews on gossip columnist, Joyce Haber.

❦

You have to have a stomach for ugliness to endure Carol Kane – to say nothing of the zombie-like expressions she mistakes for acting.

John Simon

❦

She was divinely, hysterically, insanely malevolent.

Bette Davis on Theda Bara

❦

Tallulah Bankhead barged down the Nile last night as Cleopatra and sank.

John Mason Brown

❦

I'm as pure as the driven slush.

Tallulah Bankhead

❦

Not since Attila the Hun swept across Europe leaving 500 years of total blackness has there been a man like Lee Marvin.

Josh Logan

❦

He hasn't got enough sense to bore assholes in wooden hobbyhorses.

Dorothy Parker on a Hollywood producer

❦

If you say, 'Hiya, Clark, how are you?' He's stuck for an answer.

Ava Gardner on Clark Gable

❦

The man was a major comedian, which is to say that he had the compassion of an icicle, the effrontery of a carnival shill, and the generosity of a pawn broker.

S. J. Perelman on Groucho Marx

❦

One of the most characteristic sounds of the
English Sunday morning is [the critic] Harold
Hobson barking up the wrong tree.

Penelope Gilliatt

It is disappointing to report that George Bernard Shaw appearing as George Bernard Shaw is sadly miscast in the part. Satirists should be heard and not seen.

Robert Sherwood

<hr>

Reviewing has one advantage over suicide: in suicide you take it out of yourself; in reviewing you take it out of other people.

George Bernard Shaw

<hr>

A dramatic critic is a man who leaves no turn unstoned.

George Bernard Shaw

<hr>

Has anyone ever seen a drama critic in the daytime? Of course not. They come out after dark, up to no good.

P. G. Wodehouse

<hr>

Olivier brandished his technique like a kind of stylistic alibi. In catching the eye, he frequently disengaged the brain.

Russell Davies on Sir Laurence Olivier

His voice is something between bland and grandiose: blandiose perhaps.

Kenneth Tynan on Sir Ralph Richardson

Miss Massey, with her puffed cheeks and popping eyes, is torn between ham and hamster – for the more technique she pours into this tiny role the more it overflows into melodrama.

Alan Brien, The Spectator, *on Anna Massey*

The sum total is considerably less than the parts.

Variety *on* Goodbye Mr Chips

He acts like he's got a Mixmaster up his ass and doesn't want anyone to know it.

Marlon Brando on Montgomery Clift

⁂

An empty taxi stopped and Jack Warner got out.

Anon

⁂

They shot too many pictures and not enough actors.

Walter Winchell

⁂

As camp as a Boy Scout jamboree, and as corny as a chiropodists' convention.

Film Review on Strictly Ballroom

⁂

Diane Keaton . . . is yet another of those non-actresses this country produces in such abundance – women who trade on the raw materials of their neuroses, which has nothing to to with acting . . . . Her work, if that is the word for it, always consists chiefly of dithering, blithering, neurotic coming apart at the seams – an acting style that is really a nervous breakdown in slow-motion.

John Simon

∽◈∾

Most of it is so slowly paced you could not only pour yourself a drink between the lines of dialogue, but add ice too.

Evening Standard *on* Shaft's Big Score

∽◈∾

Charlotte Rampling – a poor actress who mistakes creepiness for sensuality.

John Simon

∽◈∾

If you smeared Germolene over those lips, his mouth would heal over.

Anon on Kenneth Branagh

❦

A sort of cockney Ivy Compton-Burnett.

Noël Coward on Harold Pinter

❦

For the eye, too much; for the ear, too little; for the mind, nothing at all.

Bernard Levin on Franco Zeffirelli's Othello

❦

One of those inexplicable farces which capture the hearts of countless London-goers, despite plots of appalling banality and dialogue that writers of cat-food commercials might well spurn.

Sheridan Morley on No Sex Please – We're British

❦

MEDIA

Joan Collins is a commodity who would sell her own bowel movements.

Anthony Newley (ex-husband)

❧❧❧

When it comes to acting, Joan Rivers has the range of a wart.

Stewart Klein

❧❧❧

The closest thing to Roseanne Barr's singing the national anthem was my cat being neutered.

Johnny Carson

❧❧❧

I must say I find television very educational. The minute somebody turns it on, I go to the library and read a good book.

Groucho Marx

❧❧❧

Television: the bland leading the bland.

Anon

❧❧❧

Radio: death in the afternoon and into the night.

Arthur Miller

✧

Radio: the triumph of illiteracy.

John Dos Passos

✧

Radio is a bag of mediocrity where little men
with carbon minds wallow in sluice of their own
making.

Fred Allen

✧

Television is a device that permits people who
haven't anything to do to watch people who can't
do anything.

Fred Allen

✧

Television – a medium. So called because it is
neither rare nor well done.

Ernie Kovaks

✧

My father hated radio and could not wait for television to be invented so that he could hate that too.

Peter de Vries

I never watch the Dinah Shore Show – I'm a diabetic.

Oscar Levant

Hill's biggest defect was surely not his sexism, but the fact that he repeated himself ad nauseam.

Christopher Tookey, Sunday Telegraph, *on Benny Hill*

⚜

. . . morally and intellectually he is not fit to run a suburban cinema, let alone a TV channel enjoying privileged access to the airwaves and watched by millions.

Paul Johnson on Michael Grade

⚜

Television is for appearing on – not for looking at.

Noël Coward

⚜

Television is an invention that permits you to be entertained in your living room by people you wouldn't have in your room.

David Frost

⚜

Television: chewing gum for the eyes.

Frank Lloyd Wright

⤳⧫⤶

Journalism justifies its own existence by the great
Darwinian principle of the survival of the vulgarist.

Oscar Wilde

⤳⧫⤶

Freedom of the press is limited to those who own one.

A. J. Liebling

❧❧❧

Journalism is organized gossip.

Edward Eggleston

Most rock journalism is people who can't write
interviewing people who can't talk for people who
can't read.

Frank Zappa

Journalism is the ability to meet the challenge of
filling space.

Rebecca West

The interview is an intimate conversation between
journalist and politician wherein the journalist
seeks to take advantage of the garrulity of the
politician and the politician of the credulity of the
journalist.

Emery Kelen

The press can be best compared to haemorrhoids.

Gareth Davies

There is much to be said in favour of modern journalism. By giving us the opinions of the uneducated, it keeps us in touch with the ignorance of the community.

Oscar Wilde

Nigel Pratt-Dempster the famous social climber.

Private Eye *on Nigel Dempster, gossip columnist,* Daily Mail

He looks rather like King Edward – the potato,
not the monarch.

Anon on Ian Hislop, Editor of Private Eye

❧❧❧

Once a newspaper touches a story, the facts are lost
forever, even to the protagonists.

Norman Mailer, Esquire

❧❧❧

The man's charm is lethal. One minute he's
swimming along with a smile, then snap! There's
blood in the water. Your head's gone.

John Barry on Rupert Murdoch

❧❧❧

No self-respecting dead fish would want to be
wrapped in a Murdoch newspaper, let alone work
for it.

George Royko

❧❧❧

FINE ART &
LITERATURE

Abstract art? A product of the untalented, sold by the unprincipled to the utterly bewildered.

Al Capp

A living is made by selling something everybody needs at least once a year. And a million is made by producing something that everybody needs every day. You artists produce something nobody needs at any time.

Thornton Wilder, The Matchmaker

A little more of the abstract art and we'd both have gone potty. What is there to bite on in the abstract? You might as well eat triangles and go to bed with a sewing machine.

Joyce Cary, The Horse's Mouth

The only genius with an IQ of 60.

Gore Vidal on Andy Warhol

Who among us has not gazed at a painting of Jackson Pollock's and thought: 'What a piece of crap'?

Rob Long, Modern Review

❧❦❧

' . . . what confronts us after the first room, is a succession of increasingly vapid decorations in which the fairy-tale elements of Walt Disney spectaculars jostle utterly conventional still lives that would never have roused the Selection Committee of the Royal Academy from post-prandial slumber.

Brian Sewell on an exhibition of work by Georgia O'Keeffe

❧❦❧

All an artist needed to get into the Royal Academy was a very bad picture.

Walter Sickert

❧❦❧

I regard the Surrealists as 100 per cent fools.

Sigmund Freud

❧❦❧

Degas is nothing but a peeping Tom, behind the coulosses, and among the dressing-rooms of the ballet dancers, noting only the travesties on fallen debased womanhood.

Churchman *pamphlet*

❧

I wouldn't have that hanging in my home. It would be like living with a gas leak.

Dame Edith Evans on anon painting

❧

Usual modern collection:
Wilson Steer, water in water-colour;
Mattew Smith, victim of the crime of slaughter
 colour;
Utrillo, whitewashed wall in mortarcolour,
Matisse, odalisque in scortacolour;
Picasso, spatchcock horse in tortacolour;
Rouault, perishing Saint in thoughtacolour;
Epstein, Leah in waiting for Jacob in
 squawtacolour.

Joyce Cary, The Horse's Mouth

❧

She has the smile of a woman who has just dined off her husband.

Lawrence Durrell on the Mona Lisa

∽◦◦∾

He bores me. He ought to have stuck to his flying machines.

Auguste Renoir on Leonardo da Vinci

∽◦◦∾

My dear Whistler, you leave your pictures in such a crude sketchy state. Why don't you ever finish them?

Frederic Leighton

My dear Leighton, why do you ever begin yours?

James Whistler

∽◦◦∾

There has been nothing like this outbreak of Philistinism since Whistler's day.

Roger Fry on Post-Impressionism

∽◦◦∾

If the old masters had labelled their fruit, one wouldn't be so likely to mistake pears for turnips.

Mark Twain

❧❦❧

Bit of nonsense.

Sir Alfred Munnings on the Royal Academy Summer Show

❧❦❧

It represented the narrow and obscure taste of contemporary art mafia, out of touch with mainstream art and taste, obscure, self-serving and of dubious merit.

Independent *on the Turner Prize*

❧❦❧

It makes me look as if I was straining a stool.

Winston Churchill on portrait by Graham Sutherland

❧❦❧

There's a wonderful family called Stein,
There's Gert and there's Epp and there's Ein;
Gert's poems are bunk,
Epp's statues are junk,
And no one can understand Ein.

Anon

&

Poetry is a religion without hope.

Jean Cocteau

&

Travellers, poets and liars are all of one
significance.

Richard Braithwaite, The English Gentleman

&

I know that poetry is indispensable, but to what I
could not say.

Jean Cocteau

&

A miserable, masturbating old drunk who railed against 'niggers' and 'wogs'.

'The Weasel', Independent Magazine, *on Philip Larkin*

⤜⤛⤜⤛

All bad poetry springs from genuine feelings.

Oscar Wilde

⤜⤛⤜⤛

Blank verse, *n*. Unrhymed iambic pentameters – the most difficult kind of English verse to write acceptably; a kind, therefore, much affected by those who cannot acceptably write any kind.

Ambrose Bierce

⤜⤛⤜⤛

It would be an advantage to the literary world if most writers stopped writing entirely.

Fran Lebowitz

⤜⤛⤜⤛

If you gave Ted Hughes' much mulled-over Shakespearean fantasy to a re-write team of Judith Krantz and Umberto Eco, something like this hybrid monster would result . . . a bucketful of ludicrous tripe concocted by a prankster, marketed by cynics and aimed at (largely male) readers who crave an airport-bookstall fix with a patina of science and no giveaway glitter on the cover.

Boyd Tonkin, Observer

Filth. Nothing but obscenities.

Joseph Conrad on D. H. Lawrence

What is a writer but a schmuck with a typewriter!

Jack Warner

സാരം

As a writer he has mastered everything except language; as a novelist he can do everything except tell a story: as an artist he is everything except articulate.

Oscar Wilde on George Meredith

സാരം

Free verse is like free love; it is a contradiction in terms.

G. K. Chesterton

സാരം

The celebrated mouldy fig.

Clive Davis, Literary Review, *on Philip Larkin*

സാരം

One should not be too severe on English novelists, they are the only relaxation of the intellectually unemployed.

Oscar Wilde

All writers are vain, selfish and lazy, and at the very bottom their motives are a mystery.

George Orwell

❧❧❧

One reason the human race has such a low opinion of itself is that it gets so much of its wisdom from writers.

Wilfrid Sheed

❧❧❧

If you can't annoy somebody, there's little point in writing.

Kingsley Amis

❧❧❧

Bunyan spent a year in prison, Coleridge was a drug addict, Poe was an alcoholic, Marlowe was killed by a man he was trying to stab, Pope took a large sum of money to keep a woman's name out of a vicious satire and then wrote it so that she could be recognized anyway, Chatterton killed himself, Somerset Maugham was so unhappy in his final thirty years that he longed for death ... do you still want to be a writer?

Bennett Cerf

Writing is not a profession, but a vocation of unhappiness.

Georges Simenon

⤮⤮⤮

As a work of art it has the same status as a long conversation between two not very bright drunks.

Clive James on Princess Daisy, *by Judith Krantz*

'Thomas the Wank Engine.'

Private Eye *on* Memories and Hallucinations *by D. M. Thomas*

❧

I would sooner read a timetable or a catalogue than nothing at all. They are much more interesting than half the novels written.

W. Somerset Maugham

❧

As repressed sadists are supposed to become policemen or butchers so those with irrational fear of life become publishers.

Cyril Connolly

❧

One day we shall strangle the last publisher with the entrails of the last literary agent.

David Mercer

❧

You can trust André Deutsch as far as you can throw George Weidenfeld.

The Wit of Publishing

∾⊶⊷∾

Publishing is not a very difficult business – most people are so bad at it that it is very easy to look good.

Colin Haycraft

∾⊶⊷∾

I could show you all society poisoned by this class of person – a class unknown to the ancients – who not being able to find any honest occupation, be it manual labour or service, and unluckily knowing how to read and write, steal our manuscripts, falsify them and sell them.

Voltaire on publishers

∾⊶⊷∾

If Jane Austen were alive today she'd probably be writing books called things like *Sex and Sensibililty* and *Pride and Passion*.

Julie Burchill, Modern Review

∾⊶⊷∾

I should much rather be even a minor character in a Jane Austen novel than a major figure in an Iris Murdoch one.

Malcolm Muggeridge, Things Past

ᚬᚬᚬᚬ

He looked, I decided, like a letter delivered to the wrong address.

Malcolm Muggeridge on Evelyn Waugh

ᚬᚬᚬᚬ

It would be a relief to dig him up and throw stones at him.

George Bernard Shaw on William Shakespeare

If I didn't have writing, I'd be running down the street hurling grenades in people's faces.

Paul Fussell

❦

Her work is poetry; it must be judged as poetry, and all the weaknesses of poetry are inherent in it.

New York Evening Post *on* To the Lighthouse, *Virginia Woolf*

❦

Owen's tiny corpus is perhaps the most over-rated poetry in the twentieth century.

Craig Raine on Wilfred Owen

❦

Thomas was an outstandingly unpleasant man, who cheated and stole from his friends and peed on their carpets.

Kingsley Amis on Dylan Thomas

❦

Poets, like whores, are only hated by each other.

William Wycherley

❦

Of all the writers we have perused, Walt Whitman is the most silly, the most blasphemous, and the most disgusting.

Literary Gazette

⤜⤛⤜⤛

A poet more than thirty years old is simply an overgrown child.

H. L. Mencken

⤜⤛⤜⤛

He is like someone on a quiz show who insists on giving answers in greater detail than is actually necessary.

William Leith, Sunday Correspondent, *on Anthony Burgess*

⤜⤛⤜⤛

Good career move.

Gore Vidal on Truman Capote's death

⤜⤛⤜⤛

Her stories are puzzles, not novels. The characters aren't even lifelike enough to be caricatures. I don't like Agatha Christie at all.

Ruth Rendell on Agatha Christie

❧∾ᕫ∾☙

Wrong's title is an all-too-accurate description of its content.

Quill Quire on Wrong *by Ruth Rendell*

❧∾ᕫ∾☙

Off-form, he can be smug, sexist and narky! Surrey with a whinge on top.

Julie Burchill, Sunday Times, *on Dick Francis*

❧∾ᕫ∾☙

A tireless purveyor of romance and now a gleaming telly-figure with a Niagara of jabber, and the white creamy look of an animated meringue.

Arthur Marshall on Barbara Cartland.

❧∾ᕫ∾☙

Mr Dickens writes too often and too fast. If he persists much longer in this course, it requires no gift of prophecy to foretell his fate – he has risen like a rocket, and he will come down like a stick.

Anon, on Pickwick Papers *by Charles Dickens*

INFLAMMATORY

The white race is the cancer of all human history.
It is the white race and it alone, its ideologies
and inventions, which eradicate autonomous
civilizations wherever it spreads, which has upset
the ecological balance of the planet which now
threatens the very existence of life itself.

Susan Sontag, Partisan Review

All those who are not racially pure are mere chaff.

Adolf Hitler, Mein Kampf

I'm prepared to take advice on leisure from Prince
Philip. He's a world expert on leisure. He's been
practising for most of his adult life.

Neil Kinnock, Western Mail

The idea of Prince Charles conversing with
vegetables is not quite so amusing when you
remember that he's had plenty of practice chatting
to members of his own family.

Jaci Stephens, The Sunday Times

She is a lady short on looks, absolutely deprived of any dress sense, has a figure like a Jurassic monster . . . very greedy when it comes to loot, no tact and wants to upstage everyone else.

Sir Nicholas Fairbairn, Independent, *on the Duchess of York*

⤞⊙⊙⊙⤝

Aristocrats spend their childhood being beaten by nannies and their later years murdering wildlife, so it's hardly surprising their sex lives are a bit cock-eyed.

Jilly Cooper, Men and Super Men

⤞⊙⊙⊙⤝

An aristocracy in a republic is like a chicken whose head has been cut off: it may run about in a lively way, but in fact it is dead.

Nancy Mitford, Noblesse Oblige

⤞⊙⊙⊙⤝

I've been offered titles, but I think they get one into disreputable company.

George Bernard Shaw

⤞⊙⊙⊙⤝

Love is the victim's response to the rapist.

Ti-Grace Atkinson

❦

A hippie wears his hair long like Tarzan, walks like Jane, and smells like Cheetah.

Buster Crabbe

❦

I always say that the best years of a woman's life are the ten years between thirty and thirty-one.

Anon

❦

A woman's preaching is like a dog's walking on his hind legs: it is not done well, but you are surprised to find it done at all.

Samuel Johnson

❦

After three days fish and guests stink.

John Lyle

❦

I thought men like that shot themselves.

King George V

❧⦿❧

We invite people like that to tea, but we don't marry them.

Lady Chetwode on her future son-in-law, John Betjeman

❧⦿❧

The British middle class has always imagined that
it's enough just to be British and middle class.

A. A. Gill, Tatler

⌘

If you are an author and give one of your books to
a member of the upper class, you must never expect
him to read it.

Paul Fussell

⌘

What is the matter with the poor is poverty; what
is the matter with the rich is uselessness.

George Bernard Shaw

⌘

It is the wretchedness of being rich that you have
to love rich people.

Logan Pearsall Smith

⌘

Every man thinks God is on his side. The rich and
powerful know he is.

Jean Anouilh

⌘

The middle class has made society a public
company. Anyone can buy the shares.

A. A. Gill, Tatler

In the middle classes, where the segregation of the
artificially limited family in its little brick box is
horribly complete, bad manners, ugly dresses,
awkwardness, cowardice, peevishness and all the
pretty vices of unsociability flourish like
mushrooms in a cellar.

George Bernard Shaw

God must hate the common people, because he
made them so common.

Philip Wylie

The classes that wash most are those that work
least.

G. K. Chesterton

The middle classsses are being brave. We've got our brave little-soldier faces on. Not only is half-term cancelled but so are summer holidays, skiing in the New Year, nights at the opera, visits to the tailor, dentists in Harley Street and a part-time gardener. The middle classes just can't afford to be middle class any more.

A. A. Gill, Tatler

Each class preaches the importance of those virtues it need not exercise. The rich harp on the value of thrift, the idle grow eloquent over the dignity of labour.

Oscar Wilde

⤳⧆⤶

We're all anti-royalist and anti-patriarch, 'cos it's 1989. Time to get real. When the ravens leave the Tower, England shall fall they say. We want to be there shooting the ravens.

Ian Brown

⤳⧆⤶

The British people prefer their royalty stupid, selfish and greedy. The more ridiculous and philistine they are, the easier it is to identify with them.

Paul Foot, Sunday Correspondent

⤳⧆⤶

Men are generally more careful of the breed of their horses and dogs than of their children.

William Penn

⤳⧆⤶

A child is a curly, dimpled lunatic.

Ralph Waldo Emerson

&c<o><o>&

I like children. If they're properly cooked.

W. C. Fields

&c<o><o>&

Insanity is hereditary; you can get it from your children.

Sam Levenson

&c<o><o>&

Children should neither be seen nor heard from –
ever again.

W. C. Fields

&c<o><o>&

I think they should put the cigarette smokers and
babies together and see who drives the other crazy
quicker.

John Simon on children in aeroplanes

&c<o><o>&

I love children, especially when they cry, for then someone takes them away.

Nancy Mitford

❧

The first half of our life is ruined by our parents and the second half by our children.

Clarence Darrow

❧

Like its politicians and its wars, society has the teenagers it deserves.

J. B. Priestley

❧

Having a family is like having a bowling alley installed in your brain.

Martin Mull

❧

What is youth except a man or a woman before it is ready or fit to be seen?

Evelyn Waugh

❧

Youth is a wonderful thing. What a crime to waste it on children.

George Bernard Shaw

There are three terrible ages of childhood – 1 to 10, 10 to 20, and 20 to 30.

Cleveland Amory

Go back to school, you little nose-picker.

W. C. Fields

❦

My children weary me. I can only see them as
defective adults: feckless, destructive, frivolous,
sensual, humourless.

Evelyn Waugh

❦

Children are never too tender to be whipped. Like
tough beefsteaks, the more you beat them, the
more tender they become.

Edgar Allan Poe

❦

Childhood, *n.* The period of human life
intermediate between the idiocy of infancy and
the folly of youth – two removes from the sin of
manhood and three from the remorse of age.

Ambrose Bierce

❦

What is more enchanting than the voices of young people when you can't hear what they say?

Logan Pearsall Smith

❧

Children make the most desirable opponents in *Scrabble* as they are both easy to beat and fun to cheat.

Fran Lebowitz

❧

SPORT

Serious sport has nothing to do with fair play. It is bound up with hatred, jealousy, boastfulness, disregard of all rules and sadistic pleasure in witnessing violence: in other words it is war minus the shooting.

George Orwell

❧❧❧

Baseball has the great advantage over cricket of being sooner ended.

George Bernard Shaw

❧❧❧

This exciting sport got its start as a symptom of mental illness in northern climes such as Norway and Sweden . . .. Americans did very little ski jumping until the television programme *Wide World of Sports* began showing a promotional film snippet in which a ski jumper hurtles off the edge of the chute, completely out of control with various organs flying out of his body. Fitness buffs saw this and realized that any activity with such great potential for being fatal must be very good for you, so the sport began to catch on.

Dave Barry, Stay Fit and Healthy until You're Dead

❧❧❧

Golf is a good walk spoiled.

Mark Twain

❦

Skiing? Why break my leg at 40 degrees below zero when I can fall downstairs at home?

Corey Ford

❦

Golf: a game in which you claim the privileges of age, and retain the playthings of childhood.

Samuel Johnson

❦

I regard golf as an expensive way of playing marbles.

G. K. Chesterton

❦

The only time he opens his mouth is to change feet.

David Feherty on Nick Faldo

❦

196

Golf is too slow a game for Canada. We would go to sleep over it.

John B. McLenan

❦

He has a face like a warthog that has been stung by a wasp.

David Feherty on Colin Montgomerie

❦

They thought lacrosse was what you found in la church.

Robin Williams

❦

Martina was so far in the closet she was in danger of being a garment bag.

Rita Mae-Brown on ex-lover Martina Navratilova

❦

Bjoring Borg . . . a Volvo among tennis stars.

Peter Freedman, Glad to be Grey

❦

I may have exaggerated a bit when I said that 80 per cent of the top women tennis players are fat pigs. It's only 75 per cent.

Richard Krajicek

<hr />

He's never going to be a great player on grass. The only time he comes to the net is to shake your hand.

Goran Ivanisevic on Ivan Lendl

<hr />

What other problems do you have besides being unemployed, a moron and a dork?

John McEnroe to a tennis spectator

<hr />

I'm not having points taken off me by an incompetent old fool. You're the pits of the world.

John McEnroe to Edward James

<hr />

Boxing is as cruel a blood sport as hunting; although the victims aren't dumb animals but poor blacks.

Michael Arditti, Evening Standard

∞∞∞

If I ever needed a brain transplant, I'd choose a sportswriter because I'd want a brain that had never been used.

Norm Van Brocklin

∞∞∞

We've been trying to get Elvis. He's been dead long enough.

Ray Foreman on next opponent for George Foreman

∞∞∞

Joe Frazier is so ugly he should donate his face to the US Bureau of Wildlife.

Muhammad Ali

∞∞∞

McEnroe was as charming as always, which means that he was as charming as a dead mouse in a loaf of bread.

Clive James on John McEnroe

❧

You can't see as well as these fucking flowers – and they're fucking plastic.

John McEnroe to a line judge

❧

It's said that swimming develops poise and grace, but have you seen how a duck walks?

Woody Allen.

❧

I was watching sumo wrestling on the television for two hours before I realized it was darts.

Hattie Hayridge

❧

57 old farts. . .

Will Carling on the Rugby Union governing body's committee

A surfer is an American lemming.

Jacob Bronowski

I failed to make the chess team, because of my height.

Woody Allen

Bereft of an original turn of phrase, dispensing clichés like election mailshots, declaiming non sequiturs of prodigious lunacy in the tones of Charlton Heston, polishing one another's egos and generally investing golf with an importance above all goings-on in this violent world, they seem devoid of all original thought . . . .

Ian Woolridge on golf, Daily Mail

Golf is a lot of walking, broken up by disappointment and bad arithmetic.

Mark Twain

❧❧❧

Sailing, *n*. The fine art of getting wet and becoming ill while slowly going nowhere at great expense.

Henry Beard and Roy McKie, A Sailor's Dictionary

❧❧❧

I don't think there's much doubt about who's the smuggest bastard among football's TV stars. Yes, it's that well-known wildlife slaughterer, Jimmy Hill ... Take that chin away to the Natural History Museum where it belongs.

When Saturday Comes

❧❧❧

When a man wants to murder a tiger he calls it sport; when a tiger wants to murder him he calls it ferocity.

George Bernard Shaw

❧❧❧

A sportsman is a man who, every now and then, simply has to go out and kill something.

Stephen Leacock

❧⟡❧

The fascination of shooting as a sport depends almost wholly on whether you are at the right or wrong end of the gun.

P. G. Wodehouse

❧⟡❧

The English country gentleman galloping after a fox – the unspeakable in full pursuit of the uneatable.

Oscar Wilde

❧⟡❧

Ballet is the fairies' baseball.

Oscar Levant

❧⟡❧

Call me Un-American; call me Canadian or
Swedish, I don't care. I hate baseball . . . I have lots
of reasons to hate baseball. For one it's dull.
Nothing happens. Watching baseball is like going
to a lecture by a member of the 'Slow. . . Talkers. . .
of America'. It's like turning on the TV . . . when
the cable is out. It's like watching grass – no,
Astro-Turf grow.

Jeff Jarvic, Entertainment Weekly

Managing a baseball team is like trying to make
chicken salad out of chicken shit.

Joe Kulel

Chess is seldom found above the upper-middle
class: it's too hard.

Paul Fussell.

Exercise is bunk. If you are healthy, you don't need
it; if you are sick, you shouldn't take it.

Henry Ford

Gambling promises the poor what property performs for the rich; that is why the bishops dare not denounce it fundamentally.

George Bernard Shaw

❧❧❧

I wanted to have a career in sports when I was young, but I had to give it up. I'm only six feet tall, so I couldn't play basketball. I'm only 190 pounds, so I couldn't play football. And I have 20-20 vision, so I couldn't be a referee.

Jay Leno

❧❧❧

Be kind to animals: hug a hockey player.

Bumper sticker

❧❧❧

The game is too long, the season is too long and the players are too long.

Jack Dolph on basketball

❧❧❧

Someone with about as much charisma as a damp
spark plug.

Alan Hubbard, Observer *on Nigel Mansell*

⤸⧽⧼⤸

I thought he was one of the human race, but he is
not.

Alain Prost on Ayrton Senna

⤸⧽⧼⤸

He is so brave, but such a moaner. He should
have 'He Who Dares Whines' embroidered on his
overalls.

Simon Barnes on Nigel Mansell

⤸⧽⧼⤸

WBA, IBF and WBO – alphabetical corporations
which currently misrule professional boxing.

Patrick Collins, Mail on Sunday

⤸⧽⧼⤸

This old dumb pork chop eater don't have a chance. From eating pork he's got trillions of maggots and worms settling in his joints. He may even eat the slime of the sea.

Muhammad Ali on Floyd Patterson

⚜

He's phoney, using his blackness to get his way.

Joe Frazier on Muhammad Ali

⚜

He's like washing-up liquid: built on hype and one day the bubble will burst.

Chris Eubank on Nigel Benn

⚜

Eubank is as genuine as a three dollar bill.

Mickey Duff on Chris Eubank

⚜

Chris Eubank arrives in the boxing ring posing and parading like a peacock, so risible that even his opponent and his opponent's corner men have to laugh . . . a preposterous pugilist.

Michael Herd, Evening Standard

⌘

A lot of boxing promoters couldn't match the cheeks of their backsides.

Mickey Duff

⌘

He was all chin from the waist up.

Frank Moran on Billy Wells

⌘

Joggers are basically neurotic, bony, smug types who could bore the paint off a DC-10. It is a scientifically proven fact that having to sit through a three-minute conversation between two joggers will cause your IQ to drop 13 points.

Rick Reilly, Sports Illustrated

⌘

L' Huomo Dull personified. Seb Coe in a C&A
V-neck is like a square peg in a round hole.

Peter Freedman, Glad to be Grey

Waddling around like a recently impregnated hippopotamus . . . Paul Gasgoigne had become a *bona fide* wobble-bottom . . . But should football finally fail him, at least there's a whole range of alternative careers now on the horizon. Father Christmas . . . barrage balloon . . . spacehopper.

Marcus Berkmann, Independent on Sunday

The human Scotweiler.

Anon on Tommy Docherty

The drunk we could all have become.

Michael Herd, Evening Standard, *on George Best*

SEX
SYMBOLS

She is so hairy – when she lifted up her arm, I thought it was Tina Turner in her armpit.

Joan Rivers on Madonna

❧❧❧

It's a new low for actresses when you have to wonder what's between her ears instead of her legs.

Katharine Hepburn on Sharon Stone

❧❧❧

A vacuum with nipples.

Otto Preminger on Marilyn Monroe

❧❧❧

She's one of the few actresses in Hollywood history who looks more animated in still photographs than she does on the screen.

Michael Medved on Raquel Welsh

❧❧❧

The only thing this actress offers us in the way of change is the constant covering up and uncovering of her charming derriere.

Judith Crist on Brigitte Bardot

❧❧❧

The Russians love Brooke Shields because her eyebrows remind them of Leonid Brezhnev.

Robin Williams

Sleeping with George Michael would be like having sex with a groundhog.

Boy George

George has always managed to keep a hairy finger on the pulse of the moneyed wally.

Melody Maker on George Michael

❧

He has turned almost alarmingly blond – he's gone past platinum, he must be in plutonium; his hair is coordinated with his teeth.

Pauline Kael on Robert Redford

❧

I knew her before she was a virgin.

Oscar Levant on Doris Day

❧

215

Working with her was like being bombed by water melons.

Alan Ladd on Sophia Loren

❧

Dramatic art, in her opinion, is knowing how to fill a sweater.

Bette Davis on Jayne Mansfield

❧

This man has child-bearing lips.

Joan Rivers on Mick Jagger

❧

She has all the emotion of a goalpost.

Anon on Linda Evans

❧

The curvaceous Bo Derek comes off as erotically as a Dresden doll.

Main Picture Guide *on Bo Derek*

❧

In his most famous role, as the gladiator, Spartacus, he had such spindly legs that he couldn't happily have carried the whole script for the epic by himself, let alone take on the whole of Rome.

Peter Tory, Daily Express, *on Kirk Douglas*

Despite her almost Nordic looks, she comes across like a bleached Jewish mother with a tongue to match.

Bob Flynn, City Limits, *on Meryl Streep*

❧❧❧

Elizabeth Taylor's so fat, she puts mayonnaise on an aspirin.

Joan Rivers on Elizabeth Taylor

❧❧❧

She is not even an actress, only a trollop.

Gloria Swanson on Lana Turner

❧✦❧

I am neither a movie star or a singer and really these days not much, other than an inflated swimsuit.

Samantha Fox

❧✦❧

... like one of those nine-year-olds from Dagenham done up in her mother's lipstick, to appear on a talent show.

Jonathan Margolis, Mail on Sunday, *on Kylie Minogue*

❧✦❧

I'm writing Kylie Minogue's biography. It's called *Superstar: Jesus Christ!*

Barry Cryer

❧✦❧

Q. What's the difference between Madonna and a Rottweiler?

A. Lipstick.

Bitch *magazine*

❧◌❧

I acted vulgar, Madonna IS vulgar.

Marlene Dietrich on Madonna

❧◌❧

That ugly, shapeless, toe-sucking slut Madonna . . . the difference between Marilyn Monroe and Madonna is the same difference as exists between Champagne and cat's piss.

John Junor, Mail on Sunday

❧◌❧

Copulation was, I'm sure, Marilyn's uncomplicated way of saying thank you.

Nunnally Johnson

❧◌❧

There's a broad with her future behind her.

Constance Bennett on Marilyn Monroe

❧◌❧

THROW-AWAY LINES

I wish I'd known you when you were alive.

Leonard Louis Levinson to a bore

You're about as useful as a chocolate teapot.

Anon

Oh my God, look at you. Anyone else hurt in the accident?

Don Pickles to Ernest Borgnine

⌾⌾⌾

The last time I saw a figure like that it was being milked.

Anon

⌾⌾⌾

Why grow around your face what grows naturally around your arse.

Anon on beards

⌾⌾⌾

I have a previous engagement which I will make as soon as possible.

John Barrymore

⌾⌾⌾

Why don't you get a haircut; you look like a chrysanthemum.

P. G. Wodehouse or W. Somerset Maugham (attributed to both)

⌾⌾⌾

If you had a brain, you'd be dangerous.

Anon

❧❧❧

A face like a wedding cake left out in the rain.

Anon, about W. H. Auden

⤜⧉⤛

She was the personification of a knitting pattern.

Isabella Forbes about a colleague

⤜⧉⤛

I *never* forget a face, but in your case I'll be glad to make an exception.

Groucho Marx

⤜⧉⤛

I'm going to memorize your name and throw my head away.

Oscar Levant

⤜⧉⤛

She's had so many nips and tucks that she now walks with her miniature beside her.

Anon

⤜⧉⤛

She got her good looks from her father. He's a plastic surgeon.

Groucho Marx

❧❦❧

You've got a body to die for, and a face to protect it.

Anon

❧❦❧

Winston, you are drunk.

Bessie Braddock, MP

Indeed, Madam, and you are ugly but tomorrow I'll be sober.

Winston Churchill

❧❦❧

What's on your mind? If you'll forgive the overstatement.

Fred Allen

❧❦❧

May you be cursed with chronic anxiety about the weather.

John Burroughs

May your sex life be as good as your credit.

J. Corigan

Is that a new hairdo or did you just walk through a wind tunnel?

Anon

The next time you wash your neck, wring it.

Anon

You're the kind of person who lights up a room by leaving it.

Anon

Excuse me. You seem to have have lost your L-plates.

Anon

⤺⧉⤐

You're a birdbrain, and I mean that as an insult to birds.

George S. Kaufman

⤺⧉⤐

The man was so small, he was a waste of skin.

Fred Allen

⤺⧉⤐

I hope you live to be as old as your jokes.

Anon

⤺⧉⤐

Is that your face or is today Halloween?

Anon

⤺⧉⤐

You have a ready wit. Let me know when it's ready.

Henry Youngman

⤺⧉⤐

He has one of those characteristic British faces that once seen is never remembered.

Oscar Wilde

❦

The only thing his conversation needs is a little lockjaw.

Anon

❦

Please turn off your mouth. It's still running.

Anon

❦

That man's voice is even louder than his tie.

Anon

❦

Only dull people are brilliant at breakfast.

Oscar Wilde

❦

You've given me something to live for – revenge.

Anon

೧ೲ

I've heard better conversations in alphabet soup.

Anon

೧ೲ

What were you when you were alive?

Henry Youngman

೧ೲ

One more wrinkle and you could pass for a prune.

Anon

೧ೲ

You look like a million dollars – all green and wrinkled.

Joseph Rosenbloom

೧ೲ

Darling, if that's a mink you're wearing, then there are a lot of rabbits living under assumed names.

Anon

❧❦❧

The way she walks about you'd think she was trying to balance her family tree on the end of her nose.

Anon

❧❦❧

If I've said anything to insult you, I've tried my utmost, believe me.

Anon

❧❦❧

If you lived by your wits, you'd starve.

Joseph Rosenbloom

❧❦❧

Have I met you someplace before? I sometimes get careless where I go.

Anon

❧❦❧

That girl's been on more laps than a table napkin.

Anon

That girl's been on more laps than a table napkin.

She has the sort of charm that rubs off with tissues and cold cream.

Anon

You'd think such a little mind would be lonely in such a big head.

Anon

Don't go away. I want to forget you exactly as you are.

Anon

If you were a building, you'd be condemned.

Joseph Rosenbloom

You're so short, when it rains you're the last one to know.

Anon

The only thing you took up in school was space.

Anon

ఆఆఆ

May you be up to your ass in alligators.

Cajun

ఆఆఆ

You must be older than you look. No one could get so stupid so fast.

Anon

ఆఆఆ

You have an hourglass figure. Pity the sand has settled in the wrong place.

Anon

ఆఆఆ

You must have a sixth sense. There's no sign of the other five.

Anon

ఆఆఆ

You keep opening things by mistake – mostly your mouth.

Anon

❧❧❧

Help prevent air-pollution. Stop talking!

Anon

❧❧❧

Please close your mouth so I can see the rest of your face.

Anon

❧❧❧

You couldn't count to twenty without taking your shoes off.

Anon

❧❧❧

If your IQ were any lower, you'd trip over it.

Anon

❧❧❧

You have the brain of a four-year-old child, and I'll bet he was glad to get rid of it.

Groucho Marx

❧❧❧

You sperm of the devil.

Paula Yates

Even your insults emenate from your genitalia.

Ian Hislop Have I Got News For You

❧❧❧

INDEX

INDEX

INDEX

245

INDEX